Gua Pi Keday

or

I Went to the Shops

Kata-kata

Vocabulary

Chrita Peranakan Baru series

New Peranakan Tales series

All Rights Reserved.
No part of this publication may be reproduced, stored in a retrieval system, or transmitted, in any form or by any means electronic, mechanical, photocopying, recording or otherwise, without the prior written permission of the publishers.

Theresa Fuller and Tim Fuller assert the moral right to be identified as the authors of this work.

Bare Bear Media

ISBN 978-1-925748-26-0 - Print
ISBN 978-1-925748-27-7 - Ebook

Cover by Helzkat Designs

Copyright August 2024©

Sincere thanks to my husband, Paul, who supported this work in every way possible. I love you.

National Library of Australia
US Library of Congress

Published 4th of September 2024

Introduction

Language is powerful.

In 2022, I started the Baba Malay Today series to rectify what I felt was a vacuum in the learning of Baba Malay. The planned three mini textbooks soon grew into 5 then 8 and is still growing. But what is the point of textbooks without readers?

Thus in 2024, I began New Peranakan Tales - a series of readers for anyone interested in Baba Malay.

This particular story came about because of a game that we play in my family.

> *I went to the market and bought...*

One member of the family starts by picking something that begins with the letter A.

> *I went to the market and bought an apple.*

Then the next member of the family continues on.

> *I went to the market and bought an apple and a banana.*

It is a game that many of you I am sure will remember. The difference here is that we will use Baba Malay words. And of course the same rules apply. Forget a word and you're out!

> Enjoy!

This is Baba Malay, the language of the Peranakans.

> **YOUR** language.

Baba Malay

Baba Malay is the language of my ancestors.

A language that I discovered late in 2021 was about to go extinct with fewer than a thousand speakers in the world. I took a course in Baba Malay taught by Kenneth Chan, author of *BABA MALAY FOR EVERYONE - A comprehensive guide to the Peranakan language*. This was my start to saving Baba Malay.

But I believed much more had to be done.

The book you hold in your hands is the result of my mad persistence to save my language. While there are books out there on Baba Malay, I found little in the way for children. As a teacher, I believe that to save a language we must start with the young.

I wanted a book that parents could give to their children.
One I could give to my kids.

This is my attempt.

Theresa, affectionately known in the Peranakan community as Bibek Theresa.

    Sydney,
    29th of May, 2022

Chobak

Chobak = To Try

The Baba Malay Alphabet

A, B, C, D, E, G, H, I, J, K, L, M, N, O, P, R, S, T, U, W, Y & Z.

22 letters

Going by William Gwee's dictionary - a baba malay dictionary - there are apparently 22 letters in the Baba Malay alphabet. I will follow this even though I have found 2 words beginning with 'F':

> Faida = Faedah (Standard Malay), Interèst (English)
> Feshen = Fashion

The first word was found in Pantun Pilihan Peranakan Baba Negeri Selat 1910-1930, edited by Ding Choo Ming while the second word was found in Shellabear's writing.

There is only one word beginning with 'Z' which is Zigoma which means to con. As it is a verb, I will leave it out.

Hence, I will only use 21 letters.

Gua Pi Keday

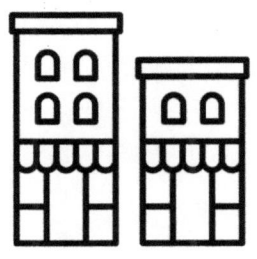

Keday = Shop

Gua pi keday.
I went to the shops.

Gua beli...
I bought...

Glossary

Beli = Bought
Gua = I
Keday = Shops
Pi = Went

Let's start!

Gua pi keday.

Gua beli alia.

Note:

The rules are simple. Each member of the group gets a turn. The first person starts off by saying, "I went to the shops. I bought alia."

Then the second person continues by adding another item. This item must start with the next letter in the alphabet and so on.

A

Alia = Ginger

Glossary

Achair = Pickles
Alagoju = Sidekick
Alipan = Centipede
Ampay = Jellyfish
Anggor = Grapes
Arimo = Tiger

Gua pi keday.

Gua beli alia, bambu.

Note:

There is no conjunction 'and'.

If you wish you may use the Malay word 'dan.'
Example below:

Gua beli alia, dan bambu.

Or just omit the conjunction altogether. The main thing is to practise, whichever way you choose to go.

Have fun!

B

Bambu = Bamboo

Glossary

Bak = Pork/meat
Bangku = Stool
Bara = Live coal
Belut = Mud eel

Gua pi keday.

Gua beli alia, bambu, chingkerek.

Note:

When my family plays this game, we often use the articles 'a' or 'an'.

Example:

I bought an apple and a banana.

But there are no articles in Baba Malay.

If you wish you could use 'satu' or 'sau' which means 'one' or 'single'. Or simply omit as I have done.

The main thing is to familiarise yourself with the words.

Chempaka according to William Gwee is the frangipani, but there are some who believe it to be the Magnolia champaca.

C

Chingkerek = Field Cricket

Glossary

Chempaka = Frangipani
Chenderawaseh = Bird of Paradise
Chicak = House lizard
Chien si = Kitchen ladle
Chinchao = Grass jelly

Gua pi keday.

Gua beli alia, bambu, chingkerek, durian.

D

Durian = Fruit of Thorns

Glossary

Dadu = Dice
Dam = Draughts
Daon = Leaf
Daway = Wire
Didair = Thimble

Gua pi keday.

Gua beli alia, bambu, chingkerek, durian, embun.

Note:

Well-done!

Memory games are tough! So great job on coming this far.

When I play this game with my little one, I let him pick where we stop. Then I congratulate him.

The main thing is to have fun!

E

Embun = Dew

Glossary

Empedair = Gizzard
Empedu = Gall-bladder
Epok-epok = Potato puff pastry
Epok Sayor = Turnip and bean pastry puff

Gua pi keday.

Gua beli alia, bambu, chingkerek, durian, embun, gajah.

G

Gajah = Elephant

Glossary

Gabus = Cork
Garam = Salt
Genteng = Roof tile
Gigi = Tooth
Gitar = Guitar
Gula = Sugar

Gua pi keday.

Gua beli alia, bambu, chingkerek, durian, embun, gajah, han cheng.

H

Han Cheng = News

Glossary

Hantu = Ghost
Hud Cho = Goddess of Mercy
Hu Ee = Fish balls
Hu Sit = Sharks fin
Huat Kueh = Chinese sponge cake

Gua pi keday.

Gua beli alia, bambu, chingkerek, durian, embun, gajah, han cheng, itek.

I

Itek = Duck

Glossary

Ikan = Fish or fishes
Ikan Aruan = Mud fish
Ikan Belodok = Goby
Injin = Engine
Istana = Palace

Gua pi keday.

Gua beli alia, bambu, chingkerek, durian, embun, gajah, han cheng, itek, jagong.

J

Jagong = Corn or maize

Glossary

Jaganan = Malay salad
Janggot = Beard
Jantong = Heart
Jari = Fingers
Jarom = Needle

Gua pi keday.

Gua beli alia, bambu, chingkerek, durian, embun, gajah, han cheng, itek, jagong, kalajengkeng.

Note:

Yay!

You are almost half-way through!

You are doing a great job!

K

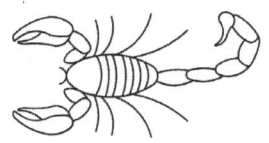

Kalajengkeng = Scorpion

Glossary

Kachuak = Cockroach
Kalde = Donkey
Kanchel = Mousedeer
Kapair = Boat
Kapak = Axe
Kayu = Wood

Gua pi keday.

Gua beli alia, bambu, chingkerek, durian, embun, gajah, han cheng, itek, jagong, kalajengkeng, lang-lang.

L

Lang-lang = Eagle

Glossary

Laba-laba = Spider
Labi-labi = Turtle
Lada = Pepper
Lampu = Lamp
Landak = Porcupine
Locheng = Bell

Gua pi keday.

Gua beli alia, bambu, chingkerek, durian, embun, gajah, han cheng, itek, jagong, kalajengkeng, lang-lang, mangga.

M

Mangga = Mango

Glossary

Machiok = Mahjong
Mata = Eye
Matoka = Car (or kereta)
Manek = Beads
Mangkok = Bowl
Mas/Mair = Gold
Meja = Table

Gua pi keday.

Gua beli alia, bambu, chingkerek, durian, embun, gajah, han cheng, itek, jagong, kalajengkeng, lang-lang, mangga, naga.

N

Naga = Dragon

Glossary

Nanas/nanair = Pineapple
Nangka = Jackfruit
Nasik = Rice
Negeri = Country
Nira Kabong = Palm sugar
Nyamok = Mosquito

Gua pi keday.

Gua beli alia, bambu, chingkerek, durian, embun, gajah, han cheng, itek, jagong, kalajengkeng, lang-lang, mangga, naga, onta.

O

Onta = Camel

Glossary

O kui thau = French Beans
Oa kan = Vase
Obat = Medicine
Otak = Brain

Gua pi keday.

Gua beli alia, bambu, chingkerek, durian, embun, gajah, han cheng, itek, jagong, kalajengkeng lang-lang, mangga, naga, onta, pisang.

P

Pisang = Banana

Glossary

Pahat = Chisel
Pais = Spicy cooked fish in banana leaf
Patong = Puppet
Pau = Chinese dumpling
Pedang = Sword
Pelita = Lamp
Petair = Firecrackers
Pia = Biscuit/pancake
Pintu = Door/gate
Pokok = Tree

Gua pi keday.

Gua beli alia, bambu, chingkerek, durian, embun, gajah, han cheng, itek, jagong, kalajengkeng, lang-lang, mangga, naga, onta, pisang, rama-rama.

R

Rama-rama = Moth

Glossary

Rachun = Poison
Raja = King
Raket = Bamboo raft
Rendang = Dry curry and meat dish
Ringget = Dollar
Roti = Bread
Rumpot = Grass
Rupiah = Coin
Rusa = Deer

Gua pi keday.

Gua beli alia, bambu, chingkerek, durian, embun, gajah, han cheng, itek, jagong, kalajengkeng lang-lang, mangga, naga, onta, pisang, rama-rama, semut.

S

Semut = Ant

Glossary

Sabun = Soap
Saoh = Anchor
Sarang = Nest
Satay = Grilled spiced meat on skewers
Sawi = Mustard (vegetable)
Selemot = Blanket
Sekolah = School
Seraykaya = Egg and coconut jam

Gua pi keday.

Gua beli alia, bambu, chingkerek, durian, embun, gajah, han cheng, itek, jagong, kalajengkeng, lang-lang, mangga, naga, onta, pisang, rama-rama, semut, tambor.

Note:

Almost there!

You can do it! I am cheering for you.

T

Tambor = Drum

Glossary
Tabuan = Hornet
Tang Kua = Candied melon
Teh = Tea
Telor = Egg
Tempe = Fermented soya bean cake
Tengkorak = Skull
Tepong = Flour
Terompet = Trumpet
Teropong = Telescope
Thor = Peach
Tikus = Rat/mouse
Tombak = Spear/lance
Tuala = Towel
Tupay = Squirrel

Gua pi keday.

Gua beli alia, bambu, chingkerek, durian, embun, gajah, han cheng, itek, jagong, kalajengkeng, lang-lang, mangga, naga, onta, pisang, rama-rama, semut, tambor, ulair.

U

Ulair = Snake

Glossary

Ubi gantang =Potato
Ubo-ubo = Jellyfish
Udang = Prawn
Ujan = Rain
Ulat = Worm/maggot

Gua pi keday.

Gua beli alia, bambu, chingkerek, durian, embun, gajah, han cheng, itek, jagong, kalajengkeng, lang-lang, mangga, naga, onta, pisang, rama-rama, semut, tambor, ulair, wasi.

W

Wasi = Money

Glossary

Wang or Wasi = Money
Wantan = Boiled or wrapped pastry filled with minced pork
Wayang = Theatrical show
Wisit = Token gift

Gua pi keday.

Gua beli alia, bambu, chingkerek, durian, embun, gajah, han cheng, itek, jagong, kalajengkeng lang-lang, mangga, naga, onta, pisang, rama-rama, semut, tambor, ulair, wasi, yo ko.

Note:

You made it!

Yay! Pat yourself on the back or do a happy dance!

I am so proud of you.

You have accomplished something GREAT!

Y

Yo ko = Mushroom

Glossary

Yap Fun = Hawker fare of rice and meat
Yu = Oil
Yu Char Kueh = Fried dough
Yo ko = Mushroom

And that's it!

Mari kita mulai!
Let's start again!
(Play the game again only this time use different words.)

Shops in my day

Growing up in Singapore, I remember being brought to the High Street to buy dresses. This was a big treat because in my day, dresses tended to be handmade. How I remember the tailor measuring me for my next dress, and how I hated the entire procedure of being made to stand still while the dress was pinned around me.

From the High Street, my mother bought me two beautiful dresses. The first was pink silk with long sleeves - very impractical for a 7-year old tomboy. The second was of blue satin.

Dresses weren't the only things that my family purchased. I remember the egg lady who carried mountains of eggs in two wide baskets suspended from a pole. She went door-to-door. My mother would place each egg in a glass of water to see if it sank or floated. Then there were the provision shops where you could buy anything from a dictionary to rice. The rice lay in sacks displayed out the front of the shop and you had the option of whichever grade of rice you wished to purchase. Today, all rice is polished but back in my day it wasn't and you had the choice of how highly polished or not your rice was.

As children we wanted the whitest rice possible but we often got half-polished rice - the reason my parents gave was because the less polished rice had more vitamins.

If you wanted to buy flour you told the shopkeeper the quantitty you needed. Not like today where you have to buy flour prepackaged. The best part was that most of what you bought would be wrapped in paper. What a win for the environment!

To organise a delivery of groceries, my mother would write out a list. I was then sent to deliver that list to the provision shop. Sometimes, they were so quick to pack the order that the provision shop boy would arrive at my door the same time I did.

Meat however would either be purchased at the wet market or a supermarket. At the wet market, my mother would select a chicken which would be freshly killed. We would wait roughly an hour for the whole process to be completed. Today I can still remember the smells of the wet market. The cages filled with chickens. The fish mongers. The wet floors that I had to navigate with great difficulty as I did not want to slip and fall. The great big wooden chopping blocks that the meat sellers would scrape down at the end of each day. The jars of kiam chye. Mounds of fresh spices. Golden yellow, rich red.

What curry were you preparing? The Indian woman would prepare the mix for you. Then wrap it all up in a dark green banana leaf.

Coconut was freshly grated. The santan squeezed out back at home.

I remember the ice-cream man and best of all the man who made ice balls. This was grated ice flavoured with rose syrup and carnation milk.

I remember being taken to the big department stores. Being shown dolls and other wondrous toys. Like all little girls, I remember saving hard to buy the dresses that my dolls needed.

It was always a special day when I had the exact amount saved in my piggy bank. I was so proud to be taken to the department store and to make my purchase.

My most favourite memory of shopping was walking down Chartwell Drive with my Kun Kun (grandfather) to buy a toy. When we arrived at the shops at the bottom, the long process of deciding which toy I wanted began. Then my grandfather would start haggling. Yes, he would bargain and sometimes the unthinkable happened. If my grandfather and the shopkeeper couldn't agree on a price then we would leave without my toy!

I still love shopping!

www.theresafuller.com

Thank you for your support!

NOTES

Baba Malay or Chakapan Baba or the Baba language was born when Chinese traders sailed down to Southeast Asia and intermarried with the local women. A mix of Hokkien and Malay, Baba Malay went into decline after WWII as many Peranakans were killed.

This is the reason why there are no Baba Malay equivalent to some words today. When in doubt English words are often used.

Another reason is language assimilation.

There are also two registers to Baba Malay:

1. Alus i.e., a refined form that women tended to speak.
2. Kasair i.e., a coarser version practised by men.

Baba Malay tended to be spoken rather than written so there are many variations in the spelling e.g.,

kreja or kerja (work)

When in doubt I referred to Kenneth Chan's *Baba Malay For Everyone - A comprehensive guide to the Peranakan language* as well as William Gwee Thian Hock's *A Baba Malay Dictionary*.

Baba Malay is also sadly considered an endangered language.

Let's do our best to change this!

Bibek Theresa

About the Author

Theresa Fuller

Theresa Fuller has always loved stories and story-telling, but it was not until the birth of her first son that she became a full-time writer. Her aim was to write stories about her culture: Southeast Asia.

Theresa was Head of Computing at various private schools in Sydney. She has also been a Higher School Certificate (HSC) Examiner and HSC Assessor. Her teaching degrees have seen her work in primary and secondary schools and at Kalgoorlie College in Western Australia.

Her first published novel in 2018 was *THE GHOST ENGINE*, a steampunk fantasy about the fictitious granddaughter of Ada Lovelace, the world's first programmer. Theresa has published two books on Southeast Asian mythology: *THE GIRL WHO BECAME A GODDESS* (2019) and *THE GIRL SUDAN PAINTED LIKE A GOLD RING* (2022).

In 2023, *WHERE CRANES WEAVE AND BAMBOO SINGS* a visual narrative textbook for children and beginner writers was published.

Coming in September 2024 - *EATING THE LIVER OF THE EARTH* - collection of the lost folktales of the mousedeer Sang Kanchel.

In 2020, Theresa lost many family members. She threw heself into researching her family history as a way to deal with her grief. This was when she discovered that the language of her ancestors - Baba Malay - was on the verge of extinction. As a writer, teacher and selfpublishing author, Theresa found herself in an unusual position - she was able to create the curriculum that was needed to help fill a vacuum.

The result is the **Baba Malay Today** series. And now the New Peranakan Tales series starting with this book!

All in aid of saving the language.

www.theresafuller.com

Thank you for your support!

More Books in the Baba Malay Today Series

Book 1 - Interrogatory Part I   SAPA, APA, MANA *or*
    WHO, WHAT, WHERE

Book 2 - Interrogatory Part II   AMCHAM, APASAIR, BILA *or*
    HOW, WHY, WHEN

Book 3 - Conjunctions   TAPI, ABIS, PASAIR *or*
    BUT, SO, BECAUSE

Book 4 - Prepositions   ATAIR, KAT, BAWAH *or*
    TOP, NEAR, BOTTOM

Book 5 - Antonyms   ALUS, KA, KASAR *or*
    DELICATE, OR, COARSE

Book 6 - Essence   CHAKAPAN BABA ATI *or*
    THE HEART OF BABA MALAY

Book 7 - Poetry   CHAKAPAN BABA PANTUN *or*
    THE POETRY OF BABA MALAY

Book 8 - Idioms   CHAKAPAN BABA IDIOMS *or*
    THE IDIOMS OF BABA MALAY

Note: In Standard Malay, the word 'hati' means the liver/heart i.e., the core. The word 'ati' in Baba Malay actually means 'liver'. Heart is 'jantong'. But phrases such 'kind-hearted' and 'evil hearted' in Baba Malay are 'ati baik' and 'ati pekong' respectively. Not 'jantong baik.' Hence, I have used 'ati' to express the meaning of the word 'essence' or the core.'

Books in the New Peranakan Tales Series

Gua Pi Keday   I Went to the Shops

Satu Tahun Jalan-jalan   A Year of Walks

Dear Reader,

Thank you for the purchase of this book.

Please help us spread the word as we try to save our language.

Bibek Theresa

Sydney, 18th of June, 2022

Want to know when my next book will be out?

Go to www.theresafuller.com

Join my newsletter!

And never miss out again.

This book is dedicated to my aunt - Low Geok Koon.

www.ingramcontent.com/pod-product-compliance
Lightning Source LLC
Chambersburg PA
CBHW041152110526
44590CB00027B/4201